D0778577

The Family Gets a Computer

Written by Ben Halpert
Illustrated by Taylor Southerland

ISBN: Hardcover - 978-0-9827968-2-5
Softcover - 978-15009536-8-3
Library of Congress Control Number: 2014915495
Published by: Savvy Cyber Kids, Inc., Atlanta, GA

To the children of the world, may your
lives be filled with safe journeys in
both physical and virtual worlds.

To my family, friends, and
Savvy Cyber Kids supporters for
their unending encouragement.

—Ben Halpert

To all those standing behind me,
who will catch me if I fall.

—Taylor Southerland

The morning started like it did everyday.
We had a good breakfast and went out to play.

My name is Tony, and I rode my bike.
And Emma my sister rode on her trike.

Then out of nowhere, up pulled a big truck.
A man in brown shorts had a box, just our luck!

UNITED
SHIPPING

"Is he coming to our house," said Emma with glee.

"Do you think it's a present especially for me?"

UNITED
SHIPP

“This package can bring all sorts of things home.

Mom says we can take it wherever we roam.”

“What is in the box?” asked Emma.
“Maybe it’s a fox?”

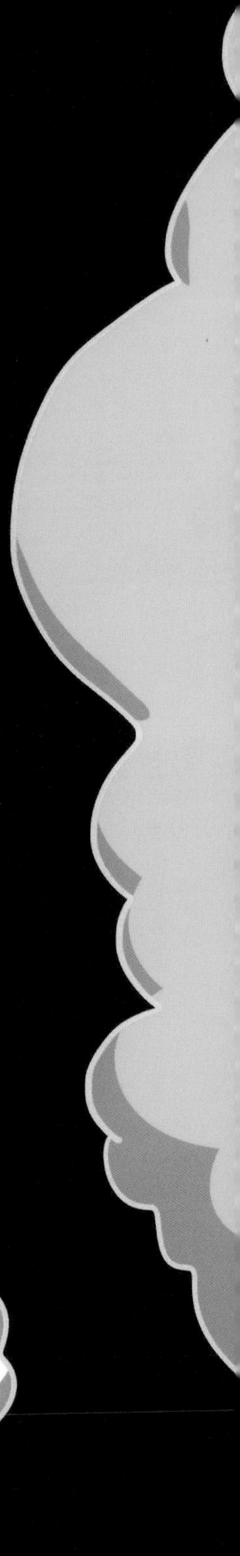

“It’s a present for all of us Emma,” said mom with a laugh and a smile. “It’s our new computer, but keep playing awhile.”

DELIVER
52 S. MOUNTAIN DR
08/15
TS 2010-14
HAPPYPC INC

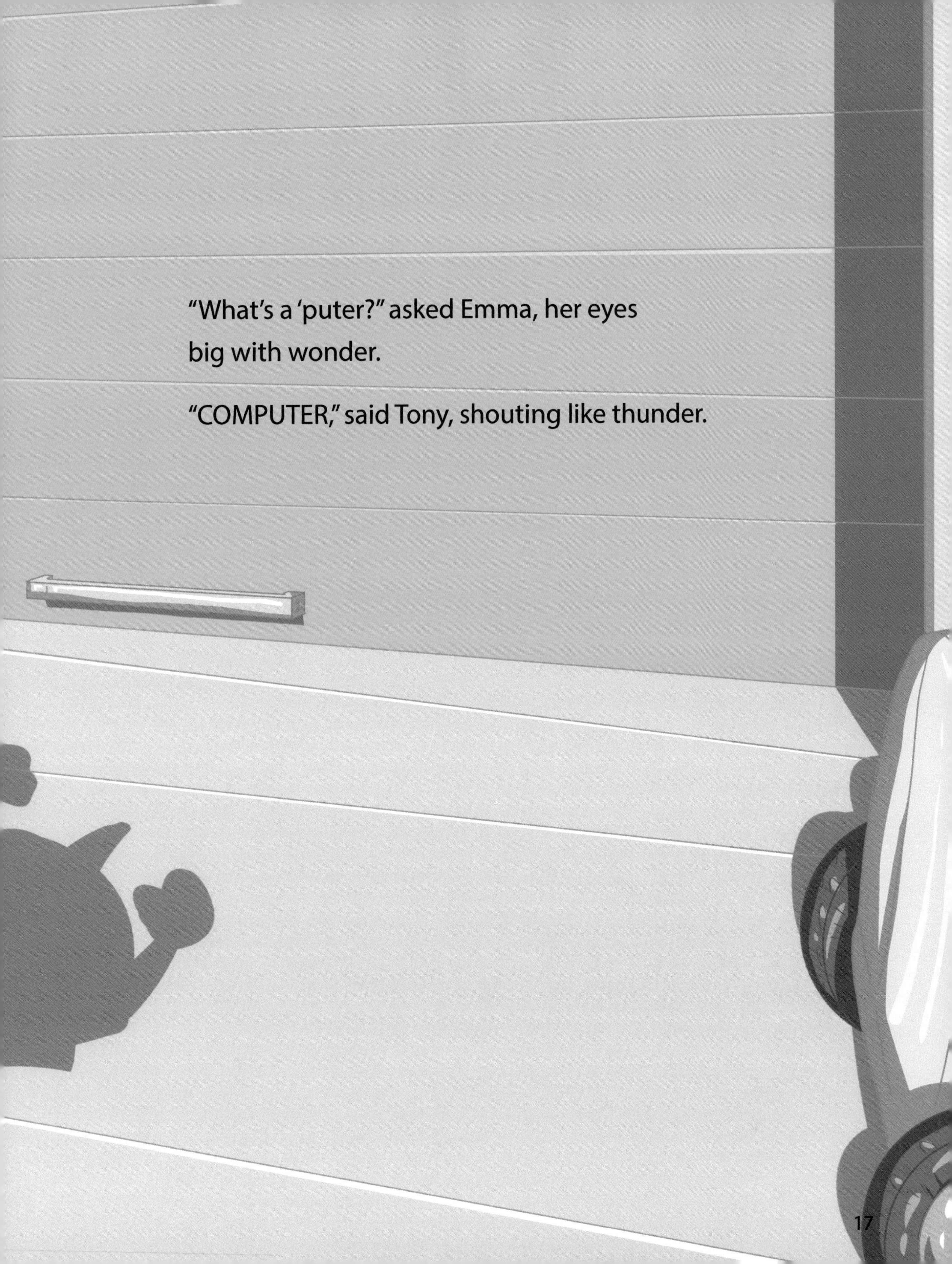

"What's a 'puter?" asked Emma, her eyes big with wonder.

"COMPUTER," said Tony, shouting like thunder.

Tony explained, "A computer is special and can do many things. Like play games, or read books, and play songs to sing."

A is for
ANEMONE
B is for
BISCUITS
I HOPE THERE'S A MOUSE!
HEY THERE'S A MOOSE!

Mom said, “Now go and play. Create your Savvy Cyber Kids names right away.”

Tony said, "We must get ready for computer play. My teacher said we have to be careful everyday."

“Be careful of what?
It is only a box.”

And with that, Emma showed
off her favorite pink socks.

Tony dressed up with a cape and
a mask. "It's important to be ready
for the day someone asks "What's
your name?" or "Where do you live?"
"Our Savvy Cyber Kid name is all we must give."

"The Internet is fun," Tony said with glee.
" Everyone has a User Name, you see. We have to be careful and safe while we play, and our Savvy Cyber Kid name keeps us safe everyday."

"Hurry up Emma,"
Tony said in a rush.

"I see you're a princess,"
he said with a hush.

"Why are you whispering?" Emma asked with surprise.

Tony said, "A stranger could be here, and our names must be disguised."

Emma said excitedly, "Well then
I will be CyberPrincess online!"

Tony yelled, "And I will be
CyberThunder and all will be fine!"

"Okay kids. The computer is ready.
Use your Savvy Cyber
Kid name and think twice.
Not all people online are nice."

SAVVY CYBER KIDS
LOGGING IN

Mom asked, “If someone wants to know your name, what will you say?” “CyberThunder and CyberPrincess is the only way!” Tony and Emma exclaimed.

Tony and Emma shouted,
"Let's go play the Savvy Cyber Kids way!
Always safe and protected online everyday!"

WELCOME
TO THE
NTERNET!

Download free activity sheets and a lesson plan at
www.savvycyberkids.org

Book 1 - The Savvy Cyber Kids at Home: The Family Gets A Computer

Book 2 - The Savvy Cyber Kids at Home: The Defeat of the Cyber Bully

Book 3 - The Savvy Cyber Kids at Home: Adventures Beyond the Screen

The Savvy Cyber Kids at Home: The Family Gets a Computer
Lesson Plan 1

Goal

To raise awareness of cyber safety issues for young children through traditional early childhood education methods including family and classroom reading opportunities, hands on experiences, and interactive learning.

Objectives

1. The student will understand the importance of being safe online
2. The student will create a Savvy Cyber Kid identity to promote safety online by not disclosing personal information to strangers

Vocabulary words

1. Savvy
2. Computer
3. Safety
4. Online
5. Cyber
6. Personal

Procedures

1. Read Aloud/Think Aloud - Starts with focus questions, while the facilitator is reading aloud, the facilitator poses questions to the kids for them to think about

2. Model for the students how you can create a safe identity for yourself – talk about hobbies, interests, favorite shows, favorite colors, etc. and then the students will create their own Savvy Cyber Kids identities with the assistance of their family member, teacher, volunteers and the facilitators.

3. Activity sheet 1 - Color male or female Savvy Cyber Kid (CyberThunder or CyberPrincess)

4. Activity Sheet 2 – Kids draw (and decorate) their own Savvy Cyber Kid and create a Savvy Cyber Kid name.

5. Introduction of students with their online identity name (Savvy Cyber Kids name) and why they chose it.

6. Review focus questions

The Savvy Cyber Kids at Home: The Family Gets a Computer

Activity Sheet – Coloring CyberThunder

The Savvy Cyber Kids at Home: The Family Gets a Computer

Activity Sheet – Coloring CyberPrincess

The Savvy Cyber Kids at Home: The Family Gets a Computer

Activity Sheet – Create Your Own Savvy Cyber Kid and Name

Savvy Cyber Kid Name: ______________________________

Draw and Color Your Savvy Cyber Kid

About Savvy Cyber Kids

The mission of Savvy Cyber Kids, a 501(c)(3) nonprofit organization, is to enable youth to be empowered with technology by providing age appropriate resources and education. Savvy Cyber Kids focuses on ingraining security awareness and ethics into the minds of children ages 3 – 7. Targeting children at the earliest of ages will enable appropriate decision making to be second nature as the child matures surrounded by a world filled with interactive technology.

LOGGING IN

CPSIA information can be obtained at www.ICGtesting.com
Printed in the USA
BVIW12n0844310117
474865BV00002B/2